REPTILES
Scaly-Skinned Animals

by Laura Purdie Salas

illustrated by Rosiland Solomon

Picture Window Books
Minneapolis, Minnesota

Thanks to our advisers for their expertise, research, and advice:

Robert C. Dowler, Ph.D.
Tippett Professor of Biology
Angelo State University
San Angelo, Texas

Terry Flaherty, Ph.D., Professor of English
Minnesota State University, Mankato

Editor: Shelly Lyons
Designer: Lori Bye
Page Production: Melissa Kes
Art Director: Nathan Gassman
Editorial Director: Nick Healy
Creative Director: Joe Ewest
The illustrations in this book were created digitally.

Picture Window Books
151 Good Counsel Drive
P.O. Box 669
Mankato, MN 56002-0669
877-845-8392
www.picturewindowbooks.com

Photo Credits: page 22 (top row, left to right, and repeated uses),
iStockphoto/Eric Isselée, Dreamstime/Liuqf, iStockphoto/Wan
Enhua, Fotolia/Madalou, Shutterstock/kkaplin, iStockphoto/George
Peters, iStockphoto/Eric Isselée, Shutterstock/Steffen Foerster
Photography, Shutterstock/Gregg Williams, iStockphoto/Le Do.

Printed in the United States of America.

 All books published by Picture Window Books
are manufactured with paper containing at least
10 percent post-consumer waste.

Library of Congress Cataloging-in-Publication Data
Salas, Laura Purdie.
Reptiles : scaly-skinned animals / by Laura Purdie Salas ;
illustrated by Rosiland Solomon.
p. cm. — Amazing science. Animal classification)
Includes index.
ISBN 978-1-4048-5526-7 (library binding)
1. Reptiles—Classification—Juvenile literature.
2. Reptiles—Juvenile literature. I. Solomon, Rosiland, ill. II. Title.
QL645.S25 2010
97.9—dc22   2009003294

TABLE OF CONTENTS

A World Full of Animals

Millions of animals live on our planet. Scientists classify animals, or group them together, by looking at how the animals are alike or different.

Six of the more familiar main groups of animals living on Earth are: mammals, birds, reptiles, amphibians, fish, and insects. Let's take a closer look at reptiles.

All reptiles have certain things in common: They are vertebrates, they have hard scales, they are cold-blooded, they have lungs and breathe oxygen, and most of them lay eggs.

What Kinds of Reptiles Are There?

There are four main reptile groups. They include the lizards, amphisbaenians, and snakes group. They also include the turtles and tortoises group, and the tuataras group. The last group is the crocodilians.

The largest group of reptiles is the lizards, amphisbaenians, and snakes group. More than 7,500 species make up this large group of animals.

amphisbaenian

Galapagos Islands
tortoise

The smallest group of reptiles is the tuataras. These lizard-like animals are relatives to a group of reptiles that lived more than 200 million years ago.

tuatara

American alligator

Tuataras are found only on about 30 islands off the coast of New Zealand. They are nocturnal. That means they sleep during the day and hunt during the night.

Bones and Scales

Reptiles are vertebrates. That means they have backbones. Reptiles also have hard scales for skin. Like your own hair and fingernails, a reptile's scales are made of keratin. A reptile's skin protects it from overheating and keeps water inside the body.

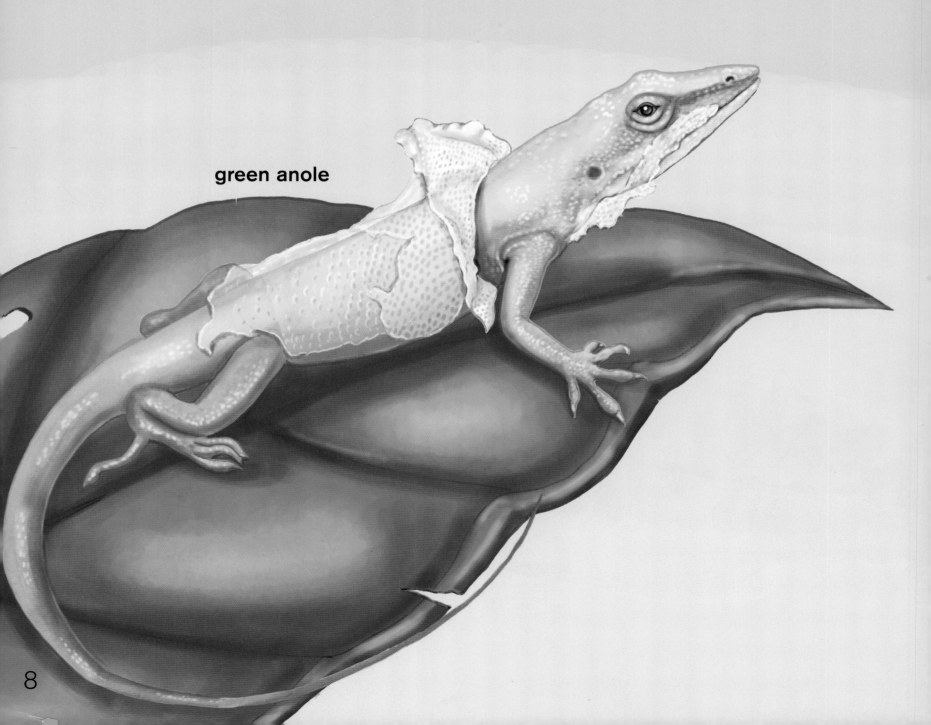

green anole

8

Some reptiles shed their skin. The old skin peels away. New skin is beneath it. Lizards and snakes shed their skin.

yellow rat snake

A snake's skin comes off in one piece as the snake slithers out of it. Lizards shed their skin in large patches or strips. Many adult snakes and lizards shed their skin several times each year. Young reptiles shed even more often.

Laying Eggs

Most reptiles lay eggs in nests. All crocodiles, turtles, and tuataras lay eggs. So do many amphisbaenians, snakes, and lizards.

sea turtle

But some reptiles give birth to live young. Pygmy lizards and boa constrictors keep their soft eggs inside their bodies. The young reptiles grow inside the eggs. After the young reptiles hatch, the mother gives birth to live young.

boa constrictors

Crocodile eggs are sensitive to temperature changes. Inside the eggs, crocodiles become males or females depending on the temperature at which the eggs are kept.

Energy and Air

Reptiles are cold-blooded. Their body temperature changes with their surroundings. They must warm their bodies in the sun. That's why reptiles, such as crocodilians and turtles, lie on riverbanks or logs in the sunlight.

crocodiles

Reptiles have something in common with human beings. They use lungs to breathe a gas called oxygen. Even reptiles that live in water breathe oxygen. Sea turtles and sea snakes, for example, have to return to the water's surface to breathe.

Some reptiles can take in oxygen from water through their skin. But most of the time, they still have to breathe oxygen through their lungs, too.

Zap, Squeeze, Bite: Hungry Reptiles

Most reptiles, such as rattlesnakes and Komodo dragons, eat meat. They might eat insects, birds, mammals, fish, other reptiles, and eggs. Some reptiles, such as sea turtles, eat both animals and plants. And a few reptiles, including some tortoises and iguanas, eat only plants.

Komodo dragons

Reptiles hunt in different ways. African chameleons zap insects with a sticky tongue. Coral snakes and beaded lizards use venom, or poison, to kill their prey. Pythons and boa constrictors squeeze their prey to death.

chameleon

All reptiles except turtles have teeth. Turtles have beaks. But most reptiles don't chew their food. They either swallow it whole, or they rip it into chunks to swallow.

Where Do Reptiles Live?

Most reptiles prefer hot, low areas to cool, high areas. They live in rain forests, on prairies, in deserts, and in the oceans. They live everywhere except near the South Pole. The red racer snake lives in the Mojave Desert. The American alligator lives in the swamps of the Everglades, in Florida. Amphisbaenians live in Africa, South America, and southern North America.

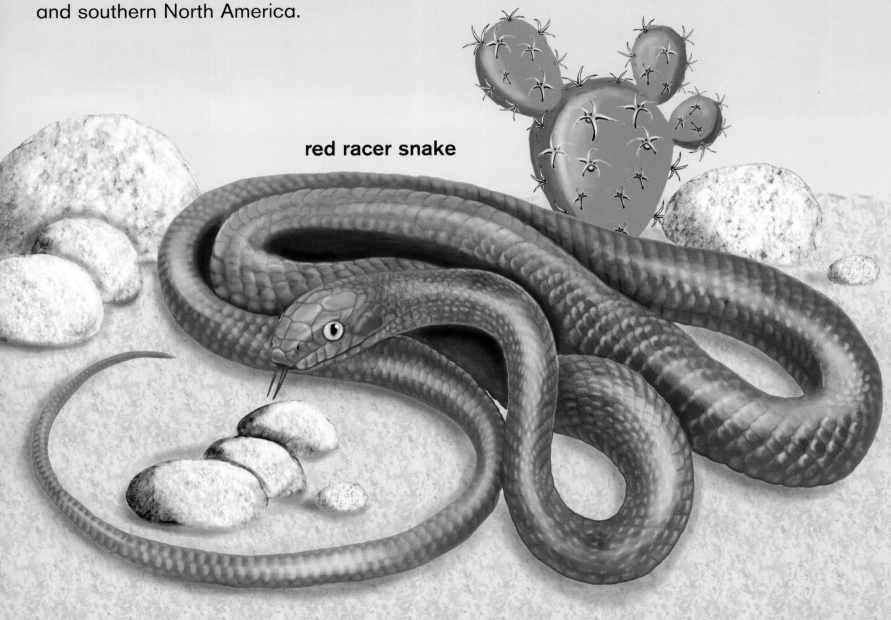

red racer snake

The bow-fingered gecko doesn't live in a hot, low area. It lives in the Himalayan Mountains, in Asia.

bow-fingered gecko

Strange Reptiles

Some reptiles look very unusual. For example, the frilled dragon has extra skin around its neck. It makes the lizard look big and scary.

frilled dragon

Other reptiles have interesting feeding habits. The African egg-eating snake can swallow eggs two to three times the size of its own head. And the Komodo dragon sometimes catches and eats goats and pigs!

Some reptiles have unusual skills. Saltwater crocodiles can stay underwater, not breathing, for more than an hour.

Reptiles in Our World

Thousands of reptiles live on Earth. They interest some people, but they scare others. Humans are more dangerous to reptiles, though. We eat them, we use their skins and shells to make things, and we put up buildings on land they need.

Reptiles do not look cute and cuddly, so not everyone cares about saving them. But reptiles do many important things. For example, lizards and snakes eat lots of insects and rats that would destroy food being grown on farms.

Some people try to protect reptiles. Laws now protect sea turtles in U.S. waters, for instance. It's important that we try to find a way to share Earth with all these amazing animals.

Scientific Classification Chart

The animal classification system used today was created by Carolus Linnaeus. The system works by sorting animals based on how they are alike or different.

All living things are first put into a kingdom. There are five main kingdoms. Then they are also assigned to groups within six other main headings. The headings are: phylum, class, order, family, genus, and species.

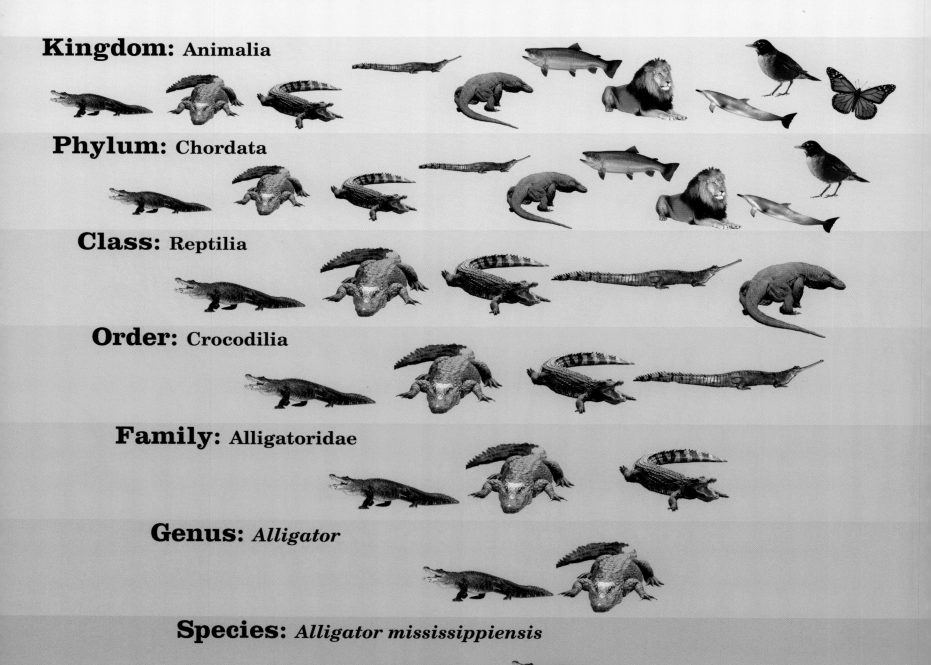

Kingdom: Animalia

Phylum: Chordata

Class: Reptilia

Order: Crocodilia

Family: Alligatoridae

Genus: *Alligator*

Species: *Alligator mississippiensis*

American alligator

Extreme Reptiles

Largest reptile: The saltwater crocodile is the largest reptile. It can grow to be more than 23 feet (7 meters) long.

Smallest reptile: A dwarf gecko called *Sphaerodactylus ariasae* that was found on a Caribbean island is the smallest reptile. It is almost 0.75 inches (1.9 centimeters) long.

Oldest reptile: Giant tortoises live the longest of all the reptiles. They regularly live to be 100 years old or more.

Fastest reptile: The spiny-tailed iguana is the fastest reptile. It has been clocked at 21 miles (34 kilometers) per hour. And a Pacific leatherback turtle swam 22 miles (35 km) per hour.

Slowest reptile: Gopher tortoises are some of the slowest moving reptiles. They usually move less than 1 mile (1.6 km) per hour.

Glossary

cold-blooded—having a body temperature that changes with the surroundings

lungs—the organs in the chest that help some animals breathe

oxygen—a gas that people and animals must breathe to stay alive

prey—an animal that is hunted and eaten for food

reptiles—animals that are vertebrates, have scales, are cold-blooded, have lungs, and (usually) lay eggs

scales—small pieces of tough skin that cover the bodies of some animals, including reptiles and most fish

shed—to drop or fall off

species—a specific type of animal that has certain characteristics

vertebrate—an animal that has a backbone

To Learn More

More Books to Read

Mattern, Joanne. *Komodo Dragon*. Mankato, Minn.: Capstone Press, 2009.

Weber, Belinda. *Reptiles*. Boston, Mass.: Kingfisher, 2006.

Williams, Brian. *Amazing Reptiles and Amphibians*. Pleasantville, N.Y.: Gareth Stevens Pub., 2008.

Internet Sites

FactHound offers a safe, fun way to find Internet sites related to this book. All of the sites on FactHound have been researched by our staff.

Here's all you do:

Visit *www.facthound.com*

FactHound will fetch the best sites for you!

Index

Look for all of the books in the Amazing Science: Animal Classification series:

Amphibians: Water-to-Land Animals

Birds: Winged and Feathered Animals

Fish: Finned and Gilled Animals

Insects: Six-Legged Animals

Mammals: Hairy, Milk-Making Animals

Reptiles: Scaly-Skinned Animals